traditional/adapted by
Dena C. Adams and Claire Clark
long came the wind and - whew - blew them in-i-gan. Poor old Mi-chael Fin-ni-gan, be-gin a-gain.

There was an old man named Mi-chael Fin-ni-gan. He raked leaves in-to the bin-a-gi

long came the wind and whish- made them swish-i-gan. Poor old Mi-chael Fin-ni-gan, be-gin-a-gain.

There was an old man named Mi-chael Fin-ni-gan. Built a dock of stone and tin-a-gi

- long came the wind and - shweee - it fell in-i-gan. Poor old Mi-chael Fin-ni-gan, be-gin a-gain.

There was an old man named Mi-chael Fin-ni-gan. His ca-noe was way too thin-a-gin

- long came the wind and - whoosh - tipped him in-i-gan. Poor old Mi-chael Fin-ni-gan, be-gin a-gain.

There was an old man named Mi-chael Fin-ni-gan. Tried to play the vi-o-lin-a-gir

-long came the wind and-whooo- broke the string-i-gan. Poor old Mi-chael Fin-ni-gan, be-gin a-gain.

There was an old man named Mi-chael Fin-ni-gan. He went dan-cing with his kin-a-gin

long came the wind and -whissst- they did spin-i-gan. Poor old Mi-chael Fin-ni-gan, be-gin a-gain.

There was an old man named Mi-chael Fin-ni-gan. Went to bed with-out a grin-a-gi